Belle City Gifts
Savage, Minnesota, USA

Belle City Gifts is an imprint of BroadStreet Publishing Group LLC.
Broadstreetpublishing.com

Bee Happy

© 2020 by BroadStreet Publishing ®

978-1-4245-6091-2

Composed and compiled by Michelle Winger.

Design by Chris Garborg | garborgdesign.com
Edited by Michelle Winger | literallyprecise.com

Printed in China.

20   21   22   23   24   25   26   7   6   5   4   3   2   1

God encourages us in his Word to give thanks in all things. That's not a mistake. When we choose to focus on things we are grateful for, our satisfaction with life increases and we become happier people. This guided journal will encourage you to focus on things that bring life and joy, reflect on Scripture and quotes that give peace and comfort, and evaluate each day in the light of truth.

Take time to ponder the sweetness of life, and . . . bee happy!

When do you feel the happiest?

_____

_____

_____

_____

_____

_____

_____

_____

_____

_____

_____

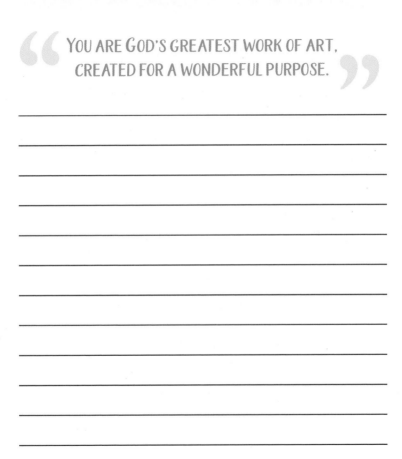

"YOU ARE GOD'S GREATEST WORK OF ART,
CREATED FOR A WONDERFUL PURPOSE."

Life is too short to be busy all the time! If you could spend the day any way you wanted to, what would you do?

_____

_____

_____

_____

_____

_____

_____

_____

_____

_____

_____

What is the best quality that
you feel you exemplify?

_____

_____

_____

_____

_____

_____

_____

_____

_____

_____

_____

WE ALL HAVE SOME REALLY GREAT MOMENTS, AND THOSE SHOULD BE REMEMBERED. WHAT WAS ONE OF THE GREATEST MOMENTS OF YOUR LIFE?

_____

_____

_____

_____

_____

_____

_____

_____

_____

_____

"For I know the plans I have for you," declares the Lord,
"plans to prosper you and not to harm you,
plans to give you hope and a future."

JEREMIAH 29:11 NIV

_____

_____

_____

_____

_____

_____

_____

_____

_____

_____

_____

_____

Write about one thing that truly inspires you.

_____

_____

_____

_____

_____

_____

_____

_____

_____

_____

_____

THE WORLD IS A BEAUTIFUL PLACE FILLED
WITH WONDER. IF YOU COULD GO ANYWHERE
IN THE WORLD, WHERE WOULD IT BE?

_____

_____

_____

_____

_____

_____

_____

_____

_____

_____

Do you know that smiling when you don't
feel like it can actually change your mood?
Write down five things that make you smile.

1. _____

2. _____

3. _____

4. _____

5. _____

What is something you are
hoping for right now?

_____

_____

_____

_____

_____

_____

_____

_____

_____

_____

LAUGH

– what can you laugh about today?

_____

_____

_____

_____

_____

_____

_____

_____

_____

_____

You don't have to be willing and able; just be willing because God is able.

Who do you feel completely loved by and why?

_____

_____

_____

_____

_____

_____

_____

_____

_____

_____

_____

Are there people in your life who really know you? What are a few things you wish people knew about you?

_____

_____

_____

_____

_____

_____

_____

_____

_____

_____

On a scale of 1 to 10, how happy do you feel today?

1 2 3 4 5 6 7 8 9 10

_____

_____

_____

_____

_____

_____

_____

_____

_____

_____

How do you find peace when everything around you feels chaotic?

_____

_____

_____

_____

_____

_____

_____

_____

_____

_____

_____

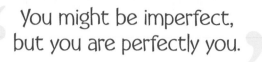

You might be imperfect,
but you are perfectly you.

_____

_____

_____

_____

_____

_____

_____

_____

_____

_____

_____

_____

I can do all this through him who gives me strength.

PHILIPPIANS 4:13 NIV

_____

_____

_____

_____

_____

_____

_____

_____

_____

_____

_____

What is the color you wear most often? Why?

_____

_____

_____

_____

_____

_____

_____

_____

_____

_____

_____

IT'S IMPORTANT TO HAVE BOUNDARIES IN LIFE.
WHAT ARE SOME THINGS YOU ARE LEARNING TO SAY NO TO?

_____

_____

_____

_____

_____

_____

_____

_____

_____

_____

_____

_____

If you could describe yourself in five words, what would they be?

1. _____

2. _____

3. _____

4. _____

5. _____

Who is the most intriguing person you have read or heard about? Why?

_____

_____

_____

_____

_____

_____

_____

_____

_____

_____

_____

It is not that we think we are qualified to do anything on our own.
Our qualification comes from God.

2 CORINTHIANS 3:5 NLT

_____

_____

_____

_____

_____

_____

_____

_____

_____

_____

_____

_____

FOCUS

– what do you need to focus on today?

_____

_____

_____

_____

_____

_____

_____

_____

_____

_____

What is your favorite childhood memory?

_____

_____

_____

_____

_____

_____

_____

_____

_____

_____

_____

THE OLDER WE GET, THE MORE WE REALIZE WE DON'T KNOW. WHAT IS SOMETHING YOU WOULD LIKE TO LEARN MORE ABOUT?

_____

_____

_____

_____

_____

_____

_____

_____

_____

_____

_____

God has
given you
everything
you need.

If you had to write a book, what would you call it,
and what would it be about?

_____

_____

_____

_____

_____

_____

_____

_____

_____

_____

_____

" If you never chase your dreams,
you will never catch them. "

_____

_____

_____

_____

_____

_____

_____

_____

_____

_____

_____

THE BOOK OF PROVERBS BY SOLOMON
HOLDS PROFOUND WISDOM.
WHAT IS A PROVERB YOU LIVE BY?

_____

_____

_____

_____

_____

_____

_____

_____

_____

_____

What is your favorite song?
What do you love about it?

On a scale of 1 to 10, how brave do you feel today?

(1) (2) (3) (4) (5) (6) (7) (8) (9) (10)

_____

_____

_____

_____

_____

_____

_____

_____

_____

_____

Use this acrostic to consider the ways
you could serve others.

S
_____

E
_____

R
_____

V
_____

E
_____

Do you find it difficult to ask for help? Why or why not?

_____

_____

_____

_____

_____

_____

_____

_____

_____

_____

_____

Family. There's really nothing quite like it. What are five things you love about your family?

1. _____

2. _____

3. _____

4. _____

5. _____

" HAVING SOMEWHERE TO GO IS HOME.
HAVING SOMEONE TO LOVE IS FAMILY.
HAVING BOTH IS A BLESSING. "

_____

_____

_____

_____

_____

_____

_____

_____

_____

_____

WHO WOULD YOU MOST LIKE TO MEET, AND WHY?

_____

_____

_____

_____

_____

_____

_____

_____

_____

_____

_____

_____

Change is a part of life. Change is what we do as we mature. If you could change one thing about yourself, what would it be?

_____

_____

_____

_____

_____

_____

_____

_____

_____

_____

_____

BLESSED

– how blessed do you feel today?

_____

_____

_____

_____

_____

_____

_____

_____

_____

_____

What can you do to bless someone today?

_____

_____

_____

_____

_____

_____

_____

_____

_____

_____

_____

What dream have you almost given up on?
Can you dare to keep dreaming?

_____

_____

_____

_____

_____

_____

_____

_____

_____

_____

_____

_____

LET GOD WHISPER
TENDER WORDS
THAT REACH THE DEEPEST
PLACE IN YOUR HEART.

What is your favorite day of the week?
Why?

_____

_____

_____

_____

_____

_____

_____

_____

_____

_____

_____

"Don't let your hearts be troubled. Trust in God, and trust also in me."

JOHN 14:1 NLT

_____

_____

_____

_____

_____

_____

_____

_____

_____

_____

_____

> **LIVE IN SUCH A WAY THAT IF SOMEONE SPOKE BADLY OF YOU, NO ONE WOULD BELIEVE IT.**

_____

_____

_____

_____

_____

_____

_____

_____

_____

_____

_____

If you had to paint a picture, what would it be of? What would you title it?

_____

_____

_____

_____

_____

_____

_____

_____

_____

_____

_____

On a scale of 1 to 10, how beautiful do you feel today?

1 2 3 4 5 6 7 8 9 10

_____

_____

_____

_____

_____

_____

_____

_____

_____

_____

WHAT IS YOUR FAVORITE THING TO DO WHEN THE SUN IS SHINING?

_____

_____

_____

_____

_____

_____

_____

_____

_____

_____

_____

_____

Write down three obstacles you are facing and then list how you can make them opportunities instead.

OBSTACLE

1. _____

_____

_____

2. _____

_____

_____

3. _____

_____

_____

OPPORTUNITY

1. _____

_____

_____

2. _____

_____

_____

3. _____

_____

_____

Priorities help you manage your time well.
What are your top five priorities?

1. _____

2. _____

3. _____

4. _____

5. _____

We all need encouragement.
What are the words you most need to hear?

_____

_____

_____

_____

_____

_____

_____

_____

_____

_____

_____

Some people love being alone.
Others thrive on being with people. How does
spending quiet time on your own make you feel?

_____

_____

_____

_____

_____

_____

_____

_____

_____

_____

_____

" IT'S EASY TO LOOK AT OURSELVES AND SEE OURSELVES AS WHAT WE ARE NOW. GOD LOOKS AT US AND SEES WHAT WE CAN BECOME. "

_____

_____

_____

_____

_____

_____

_____

_____

_____

_____

_____

What is one of the most satisfying jobs
you have done?

_____

_____

_____

_____

_____

_____

_____

_____

_____

_____

_____

_____

THANKFUL

– what are you eternally thankful for?

_____

_____

_____

_____

_____

_____

_____

_____

_____

_____

Who do you trust with your every secret?
Why do you think they are so trustworthy?

_____

_____

_____

_____

_____

_____

_____

_____

_____

_____

_____

A life of victory isn't a life without disappointment or hard work.

What does it look like to consider
yourself a citizen of heaven?

_____

_____

_____

_____

_____

_____

_____

_____

_____

_____

_____

Rejoice in the Lord always. I will say it again: Rejoice!

PHILIPPIANS 4:4 NIV

_____

_____

_____

_____

_____

_____

_____

_____

_____

_____

_____

_____

WHAT TRUTHS OF GOD CAN YOU DECLARE RIGHT NOW?

_____

_____

_____

_____

_____

_____

_____

_____

_____

_____

_____

_____

Do you need to create more margin
in your life? How can you do that?

_____

_____

_____

_____

_____

_____

_____

_____

_____

_____

_____

Words are powerful. Which five words
are among your favorites?

1. _____

2. _____

3. _____

4. _____

5. _____

What is your biggest challenge to freedom?

_____

_____

_____

_____

_____

_____

_____

_____

_____

_____

_____

> WHEN YOU CHOOSE TO LOOK AT EACH MOMENT AS A MOMENT IN WHICH TO BE THANKFUL, YOU WILL FIND IN EACH MOMENT BEAUTY, JOY, AND SATISFACTION.

_____

_____

_____

_____

_____

_____

_____

_____

_____

_____

_____

_____

On a scale of 1 to 10, how confident do you feel today?

(1) (2) (3) (4) (5) (6) (7) (8) (9) (10)

_____

_____

_____

_____

_____

_____

_____

_____

_____

_____

How do you see gentleness
affecting your daily life?

_____

_____

_____

_____

_____

_____

_____

_____

_____

_____

_____

God's Word is full of encouragement and hope.
What is your favorite Scripture?

_____

_____

_____

_____

_____

_____

_____

_____

_____

_____

_____

COURAGE
– what makes you feel brave?

_____

_____

_____

_____

_____

_____

_____

_____

_____

_____

Use this acrostic to consider the
ways you could love others.

L _____

O _____

V _____

E _____

ARE YOU HOLDING ON TO OFFENSE?
CAN YOU LET GO OF IT TODAY?

_____

_____

_____

_____

_____

_____

_____

_____

_____

_____

_____

You have so much to give! How do you participate in your community so others can see your light?

_____

_____

_____

_____

_____

_____

_____

_____

_____

_____

_____

EVERY SITUATION HAS THE POTENTIAL TO CREATE *beauty* IN YOU.

How is what you are doing right now preparing you for eternity?

_____

_____

_____

_____

_____

_____

_____

_____

_____

_____

_____

> **TODAY'S TRIAL IS TOMORROW'S TESTIMONY.**

_____

_____

_____

_____

_____

_____

_____

_____

_____

_____

_____

Most of us spend a lot of time running errands. What five errands do you run the most?

1. _____

2. _____

3. _____

4. _____

5. _____

What are you doing right now that you see God has called you to?

_____

_____

_____

_____

_____

_____

_____

_____

_____

_____

_____

Role models and mentors are critical in all stages of life. Who is the person you most look up to right now?

_____

_____

_____

_____

_____

_____

_____

_____

_____

_____

_____

"Those the Father has given me will come to me,
and I will never reject them."

JOHN 6:37 NLT

_____

_____

_____

_____

_____

_____

_____

_____

_____

_____

_____

WHAT CAN YOU DO TO START CULTIVATING A HEART OF GRATITUDE?

_____

_____

_____

_____

_____

_____

_____

_____

_____

_____

_____

_____

Laughter is good medicine.
What has made you laugh out loud recently?

_____

_____

_____

_____

_____

_____

_____

_____

_____

_____

_____

WORTHY

– where do you find your worth?

_____

_____

_____

_____

_____

_____

_____

_____

_____

_____

Do you believe God hears you when you talk to him? Why or why not?

_____

_____

_____

_____

_____

_____

_____

_____

_____

_____

_____

On a scale of 1 to 10, how hopeful do you feel today?

(1) (2) (3) (4) (5) (6) (7) (8) (9) (10)

_____

_____

_____

_____

_____

_____

_____

_____

_____

_____

GOD DOESN'T WANT YOU TO SETTLE FOR "GOOD ENOUGH." HE WANTS YOU TO GO FORWARD IN LIFE, ALWAYS PUTTING YOUR HEART AND MIND IN A POSITION TO LEARN AND GROW.

_____

_____

_____

_____

_____

_____

_____

_____

_____

_____

In which areas of your life do you need
to practice more self-control?

_____

_____

_____

_____

_____

_____

_____

_____

_____

_____

_____

Is there someone who needs your forgiveness today?
Can you put aside your hurt and offer grace?

_____

_____

_____

_____

_____

_____

_____

_____

_____

_____

_____

What can you be grateful for today? Vibrant colors, bursting flavors, moving melodies... begin there.

Do you know the goodness of God?
How have you seen it in your life lately?

_____

_____

_____

_____

_____

_____

_____

_____

_____

_____

_____

Friends are critical for healthy social development. Who are your five closest friends?

1. _____

2. _____

3. _____

4. _____

5. _____

"Be still, and know that I am God. I will be exalted among the nations, I will be exalted in the earth!"

PSALM 46:10 ESV

_____

_____

_____

_____

_____

_____

_____

_____

_____

_____

_____

_____

How do you put your hope and
confidence in God's love?

_____

_____

_____

_____

_____

_____

_____

_____

_____

_____

_____

_____

Even if you don't think so, you do have at least an ounce of creativity! What is your creative outlet?

_____

_____

_____

_____

_____

_____

_____

_____

_____

_____

_____

_____

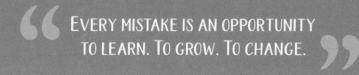

EVERY MISTAKE IS AN OPPORTUNITY TO LEARN. TO GROW. TO CHANGE.

_____

_____

_____

_____

_____

_____

_____

_____

_____

_____

_____

How do you see God's purpose
working in your life?

_____

_____

_____

_____

_____

_____

_____

_____

_____

_____

_____

Within your heart you can make plans for your future,
but the Lord chooses the steps you take to get there.

PROVERBS 16:9 TPT

_____

_____

_____

_____

_____

_____

_____

_____

_____

_____

_____

PEACE

– how can you make peace a part of your day?

_____

_____

_____

_____

_____

_____

_____

_____

_____

_____

WHEN DO YOU FIND YOURSELF MOST AT A LOSS FOR WORDS?

_____

_____

_____

_____

_____

_____

_____

_____

_____

_____

_____

_____

What is something you would like to change about yourself, or the situation you are in, within the next year?

_____

_____

_____

_____

_____

_____

_____

_____

_____

_____

_____

On a scale of 1 to 10, how strong do you feel today?

(1) (2) (3) (4) (5) (6) (7) (8) (9) (10)

_____

_____

_____

_____

_____

_____

_____

_____

_____

_____

What kind of success are you
currently pursuing?

_____

_____

_____

_____

_____

_____

_____

_____

_____

_____

_____

**Write down three areas of weakness and
then list how they can be turned into strengths.**

WEAKNESS

1. _____

_____

_____

2. _____

_____

_____

3. _____

_____

_____

STRENGTH

1. _____

_____

_____

2. _____

_____

_____

3. _____

_____

_____

WHAT IS YOUR STORY OF GOD'S WORK IN YOUR LIFE?

_____

_____

_____

_____

_____

_____

_____

_____

_____

_____

_____

Do you cherish family traditions? Have you made some of your own? What are the five family traditions that you treasure the most?

1. _____

2. _____

3. _____

4. _____

5. _____

How do you feel your faith being tested right now?

_____

_____

_____

_____

_____

_____

_____

_____

_____

_____

_____

Use this acrostic to consider
the ways you could help
someone in need.

H _____

E _____

L _____

P _____

> TRULY, YOU ARE SO MANY THINGS.
> BUT ABOVE ALL, YOU ARE A CHILD OF GOD.

_____

_____

_____

_____

_____

_____

_____

_____

_____

_____

_____

_____

Do you find it difficult to trust God in certain areas?
What are they, and why do you think that is?

_____

_____

_____

_____

_____

_____

_____

_____

_____

_____

_____

Are you afraid to be fully known?
Why or why not?

_____

_____

_____

_____

_____

_____

_____

_____

_____

_____

_____

VALUE

– what made you feel valued today?

_____

_____

_____

_____

_____

_____

_____

_____

_____

_____

Strange things happen every day. What unusual thing has happened to you recently?

_____

_____

_____

_____

_____

_____

_____

_____

_____

_____

_____

What would it take for you to see yourself as beautiful?

_____

_____

_____

_____

_____

_____

_____

_____

_____

_____

_____

Give all your worries and cares to God, for he cares for you.

1 PETER 5:7 NLT

_____

_____

_____

_____

_____

_____

_____

_____

_____

_____

_____

_____

> LIGHT. JOY. PEACE. THESE ARE THINGS THAT PEOPLE CRAVE. YOUR INFLUENCE CAN BE IN THE SIMPLE, EVERYDAY WAY YOU HANDLE YOURSELF.

_____

_____

_____

_____

_____

_____

_____

_____

_____

_____

_____

Of all the parables in Scripture, what is your favorite?

_____

_____

_____

_____

_____

_____

_____

_____

_____

_____

_____

_____

Science says that opposites attract, but that's not always true in relationships. What are the five qualities you look for most in a friend?

1. _____

2. _____

3. _____

4. _____

5. _____

Joy flows in the middle of the darkness as you trust in God's perfect ways.

When do you feel most alive?

_____

_____

_____

_____

_____

_____

_____

_____

_____

_____

_____

_____

On a scale of 1 to 10, how brilliant do you feel today?

1 2 3 4 5 6 7 8 9 10

_____

_____

_____

_____

_____

_____

_____

_____

_____

_____

_____

Who are the people in your life that fully support you?
How do they show it?

_____

_____

_____

_____

_____

_____

_____

_____

_____

_____

_____

How have you seen God move
in your life lately?

_____

_____

_____

_____

_____

_____

_____

_____

_____

_____

_____

> **GIFTS FROM GOD ARE ALL AROUND YOU. LIFT UP YOUR HEAD AND ALLOW YOURSELF TO BE INSPIRED.**

_____

_____

_____

_____

_____

_____

_____

_____

_____

_____

_____

We need to have more fun in life.
What is the most fun you've had lately?

_____

_____

_____

_____

_____

_____

_____

_____

_____

_____

_____

HOW DO YOU SHOW YOUR
LOVE TO OTHERS?

_____

_____

_____

_____

_____

_____

_____

_____

_____

_____

_____

_____

SEEK

– what are you looking for today?

_____

_____

_____

_____

_____

_____

_____

_____

_____

_____

Watch your words and be careful what you say,
and you'll be surprised how few troubles you'll have.

PROVERBS 21:23 TPT

_____

_____

_____

_____

_____

_____

_____

_____

_____

_____

_____

What is a characteristic you would love to possess, and why?

_____

_____

_____

_____

_____

_____

_____

_____

_____

_____

_____

_____

We know that joy and happiness are not the same thing. How do you have joy even when circumstances are not ideal?

_____

_____

_____

_____

_____

_____

_____

_____

_____

_____

_____

There are so many beautiful places in
this world. Which five destinations
would you most like to explore?

1. _____

2. _____

3. _____

4. _____

5. _____

Are you being honest with yourself today?
How do you really feel?

_____

_____

_____

_____

_____

_____

_____

_____

_____

_____

_____

_____

GOD'S PLAN IS BIGGER THAN YOUR PAST.

_____

_____

_____

_____

_____

_____

_____

_____

_____

_____

_____

Your message to God is never lost in translation.

What are your dreams mostly about?
Why do you think that is?

_____

_____

_____

_____

_____

_____

_____

_____

_____

_____

_____

You've heard it said a thousand times: a glass with water in it up to the middle is either half empty or half full. Do you tend to focus on the positive or negative? Why?

_____

_____

_____

_____

_____

_____

_____

_____

_____

_____

_____

This is the confidence we have in approaching God:
that if we ask anything according to his will, he hears us.

1 JOHN 5:14 NIV

_____

_____

_____

_____

_____

_____

_____

_____

_____

_____

_____

_____

HAVE YOU WALKED THROUGH A SEASON OF GRIEF? HOW DID YOU MAINTAIN HOPE?

_____

_____

_____

_____

_____

_____

_____

_____

_____

_____

_____

Take an honest look at the things you long for, dream about, and desire. What do they reveal about your relationship with God?

_____

_____

_____

_____

_____

_____

_____

_____

_____

_____

_____

On a scale of 1 to 10, how loved do you feel today?

1 **2** **3** **4** **5** **6** **7** **8** **9** **10**

_____

_____

_____

_____

_____

_____

_____

_____

_____

_____

What is something you need God's guidance for right now?

_____

_____

_____

_____

_____

_____

_____

_____

_____

_____

TRUTH

– do you know the truth deep inside your heart?

_____

_____

_____

_____

_____

_____

_____

_____

_____

What is a story you tell over and over?

_____

_____

_____

_____

_____

_____

_____

_____

_____

_____

_____

Use this acrostic to consider the ways you
could stir up joy in you and others.

S _____

M _____

I _____

L _____

E _____

We should never let our fears drive us, but to say we fear nothing is likely not true (even if we want it to be). Write down five things that terrify you the most, and then ponder whether or not those fears are rational.

1.
_____

2.
_____

3.
_____

4.
_____

5.
_____

> **DON'T JUST SAY YES. IT IS ALWAYS BETTER TO THINK CAREFULLY ABOUT A NEW VENTURE OR OPPORTUNITY BEFORE YOU COMMIT TO IT.**

_____

_____

_____

_____

_____

_____

_____

_____

_____

_____

How have you changed in the last five years?

_____

_____

_____

_____

_____

_____

_____

_____

_____

_____

_____

Who can you uplift in prayer today?
Bring a friend before the Lord in prayer.

_____

_____

_____

_____

_____

_____

_____

_____

_____

_____

_____

ABUNDANCE,
OPULENCE, SPLENDOR,
IMMEASURABLE LOVE—
it's your
inheritance!

WHAT DO YOU FIND MOST INTERESTING ABOUT PEOPLE?

_____

_____

_____

_____

_____

_____

_____

_____

_____

_____

_____

NOTHING GOOD COMES OUT OF NOT TRYING YOUR BEST.

_____

_____

_____

_____

_____

_____

_____

_____

_____

_____

May God, the inspiration and fountain of hope, fill you to overflowing with uncontainable joy and perfect peace as you trust in him.

ROMANS 15:13 TPT

_____

_____

_____

_____

_____

_____

_____

_____

_____

_____

_____

What hurts you the most?

_____

_____

_____

_____

_____

_____

_____

_____

_____

_____

_____

What are your priorities? Would they be obvious
to someone observing a day in your life?

_____

_____

_____

_____

_____

_____

_____

_____

_____

_____

_____

Write down three things you are struggling with and
then list how they could be blessings in disguise.

STRUGGLE

1. _____

_____

_____

2. _____

_____

_____

3. _____

_____

_____

BLESSING

1. _____

_____

_____

2. _____

_____

_____

3. _____

_____

_____

What is something you are
truly proud of?

_____

_____

_____

_____

_____

_____

_____

_____

_____

_____

_____

_____

CHALLENGE

– what are you challenging yourself to do today?

_____

_____

_____

_____

_____

_____

_____

_____

_____

On a scale of 1 to 10, how determined do you feel today?

1 2 3 4 5 6 7 8 9 10

_____

_____

_____

_____

_____

_____

_____

_____

_____

_____

_____

Where is your favorite place in the world, and why?

_____

_____

_____

_____

_____

_____

_____

_____

_____

_____

_____

Colors give vibrancy to the world around us.
What five colors do you love to wear and why?

1. _____

2. _____

3. _____

4. _____

5. _____

> "YOU ARE NOT A MISTAKE. YOUR HAIR COLOR, YOUR SMILE, YOUR INTERESTS, YOUR ABILITIES, THEY WERE ALL ORCHESTRATED BY THE CREATOR."

_____

_____

_____

_____

_____

_____

_____

_____

_____

_____

WHAT DO YOU GET YOUR VALUE FROM?

_____

_____

_____

_____

_____

_____

_____

_____

_____

_____

_____

Working consistently with enthusiasm can become wearying. Are you feeling drained today? What can help you push through these feelings and enjoy your day?

_____

_____

_____

_____

_____

_____

_____

_____

_____

_____

What was the best gift you ever received? What made it the best?

_____

_____

_____

_____

_____

_____

_____

_____

_____

_____

_____

_____

Refusing constructive criticism shows you have no interest in improving your life. For revelation-insight only comes as you accept correction and the wisdom that it brings.

PROVERBS 15:32 TPT

_____

_____

_____

_____

_____

_____

_____

_____

_____

_____

_____

_____

In what places, or to which people do you feel
God calling you to share his love?

_____

_____

_____

_____

_____

_____

_____

_____

_____

_____

_____

_____

_____

_____

_____

Do you find it difficult to accept
compliments? Why or why not?

_____

_____

_____

_____

_____

_____

_____

_____

_____

_____

_____

On a scale of 1 to 10, how blessed do you feel today?

(1) (2) (3) (4) (5) (6) (7) (8) (9) (10)

_____

_____

_____

_____

_____

_____

_____

_____

_____

_____

There is no fear in love. But perfect love drives out fear,
because fear has to do with punishment. The one who fears
is not made perfect in love.

1 JOHN 4:18 NIV

_____

_____

_____

_____

_____

_____

_____

_____

_____

_____

_____

_____

What do you need God to
illuminate for you right now?

_____

_____

_____

_____

_____

_____

_____

_____

_____

_____

_____

ENDURANCE

– what do you need endurance for today?

_____

_____

_____

_____

_____

_____

_____

_____

_____

_____

There are just some things we can't live without. List your top five!

1.
_____

2.
_____

3.
_____

4.
_____

5.
_____

In what ways do you need God's comfort today?

_____

_____

_____

_____

_____

_____

_____

_____

_____

_____

Submitting decisions to God and others is wise.
How do you make big decisions?

_____

_____

_____

_____

_____

_____

_____

_____

_____

_____

_____

" STAY TRUE TO YOURSELF AND KNOW THAT
WHAT GOD HAS PLACED IN YOU IS ENOUGH. "

_____

_____

_____

_____

_____

_____

_____

_____

_____

_____

_____

What do you need God to breathe life back into today?

_____

_____

_____

_____

_____

_____

_____

_____

_____

_____

_____

Put your heart and soul into every activity you do, as though you are
doing it for the Lord himself and not merely for others.

COLOSSIANS 3:23 TPT

_____

_____

_____

_____

_____

_____

_____

_____

_____

_____

_____

WEAKNESS ISN'T SOMETHING TO BE FEARED OR HIDDEN;

IT ALLOWS GOD'S POWER TO WORK IN YOU.

WHAT GIFTS HAS GOD BLESSED YOU WITH TO GET YOU TO WHERE YOU ARE NOW?

_____

_____

_____

_____

_____

_____

_____

_____

_____

_____

_____

_____

Use this acrostic to consider the ways you
could find peace in your life.

P
_____

E
_____

A
_____

C
_____

E
_____

We are told we can boldly approach God with our requests. What opportunities feel impossible to you right now?

_____

_____

_____

_____

_____

_____

_____

_____

_____

_____

_____

Where can you see God's perfection shining through your imperfection?

_____

_____

_____

_____

_____

_____

_____

_____

_____

_____

FAITH

– what level of faith do you have today?

_____

_____

_____

_____

_____

_____

_____

_____

_____

_____

Here's an age-old question that will likely never happen to you, but it's worth considering. You are going to a deserted island and can only take five things with you. What are they?

1. _____

2. _____

3. _____

4. _____

5. _____

WHAT PART OF YOUR LIFE NEEDS TO EXPERIENCE THE WARMTH OF GOD'S LOVE?

_____

_____

_____

_____

_____

_____

_____

_____

_____

_____

_____

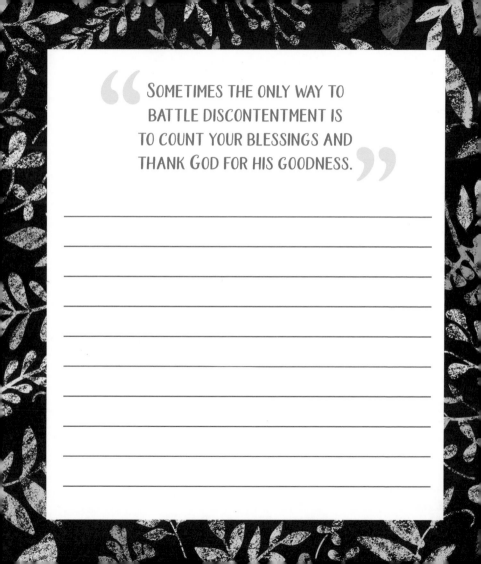

> SOMETIMES THE ONLY WAY TO BATTLE DISCONTENTMENT IS TO COUNT YOUR BLESSINGS AND THANK GOD FOR HIS GOODNESS.

On a scale of 1 to 10, how peaceful do you feel today?

(1) (2) (3) (4) (5) (6) (7) (8) (9) (10)

_____

_____

_____

_____

_____

_____

_____

_____

_____

_____

_____

What is the most relaxing way for
you to spend an hour or two?

_____

_____

_____

_____

_____

_____

_____

_____

_____

_____

_____

_____

Surprises are exciting for some and anxiety-provoking for others. Do you like surprises? Why or why not?

_____

_____

_____

_____

_____

_____

_____

_____

_____

_____

_____

The LORD directs the steps of the godly. He delights
in every detail of their lives.

PSALM 37:23 NLT

_____

_____

_____

_____

_____

_____

_____

_____

_____

_____

_____

HOW DO YOU BRING LIGHT TO A WORLD CLOAKED IN DARKNESS?

_____

_____

_____

_____

_____

_____

_____

_____

_____

_____

> STUDY A FLOWER. READ ABOUT THE HUMAN EYE. WATCH THE SUN RISE OR SET. WRITE DOWN YOUR DREAMS. SPEND SOME TIME JUST SOAKING IN THE AWESOMENESS OF THE CREATOR.

_____

_____

_____

_____

_____

_____

_____

_____

_____

_____

Let no doubt take root; God cares deeply and loves fully.

What good things are happening around you in this moment?

_____

_____

_____

_____

_____

_____

_____

_____

_____

_____

_____

What are five things that make you happy?

1. _____

2. _____

3. _____

4. _____

5. _____

God understands our weaknesses and doesn't expect perfection. What can you let go of today that makes you feel like you are failing?

_____

_____

_____

_____

_____

_____

_____

_____

_____

_____

_____

What is your favorite season of the year? Why?

_____

_____

_____

_____

_____

_____

_____

_____

_____

_____

_____

_____

WISDOM

– how can you seek wisdom today?

_____

_____

_____

_____

_____

_____

_____

_____

_____

_____

"Does worry add anything to your life?
Can it add one more year, or even one day?"

LUKE 12:25 TPT

_____

_____

_____

_____

_____

_____

_____

_____

_____

_____

_____

_____

How do you best receive love?

_____

_____

_____

_____

_____

_____

_____

_____

_____

_____

_____

> "EVERYTHING ON EARTH IS A FLEETING TREASURE, A MOMENTARY COMFORT THAT CAN BE LOST IN A FLASH. BUT THE ASSURANCE OF YOUR ETERNAL PLACE IN HIS KINGDOM IS INDESTRUCTIBLE."

_____

_____

_____

_____

_____

_____

_____

_____

_____

_____

Do you take time to really listen to others?
How could you do this better?

_____

_____

_____

_____

_____

_____

_____

_____

_____

_____

_____

WRITE DOWN YOUR FAVORITE PSALM.

_____

_____

_____

_____

_____

_____

_____

_____

_____

_____

_____

Faith is the confidence that what we hope for will actually happen;
it gives us assurance about things we cannot see.

HEBREWS 11:1 NLT

_____

_____

_____

_____

_____

_____

_____

_____

_____

_____

_____

What do you love reading about, and why?

_____

_____

_____

_____

_____

_____

_____

_____

_____

_____

_____

Write down three things you are finding difficult and
then list how those things can create beauty in you.

DIFFICULTY

1. _____

_____

_____

2. _____

_____

_____

3. _____

_____

_____

BEAUTY

1. _____

_____

_____

2. _____

_____

_____

3. _____

_____

_____

On a scale of 1 to 10, how valued do you feel today?

1 2 3 4 5 6 7 8 9 10

_____

_____

_____

_____

_____

_____

_____

_____

_____

_____

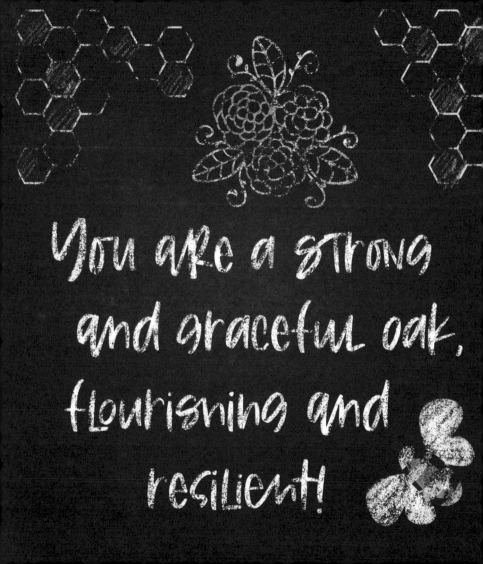

You are a strong and graceful oak, flourishing and resilient!

What is your favorite thing to do
when the sun is out?

_____

_____

_____

_____

_____

_____

_____

_____

_____

_____

_____

_____

You can't control people or circumstances, but you can control your response. What five things could steal your joy if you let them?

1. _____

2. _____

3. _____

4. _____

5. _____

If money weren't an issue, what would
you buy for whom, and why?

_____

_____

_____

_____

_____

_____

_____

_____

_____

_____

_____

Navigating our obligations in life is sometimes not much different than juggling glass inside a room of bouncing rubber balls. What are you juggling today? Can you hand it all over to God and allow him to put back in your hands only that which he wants you to carry?

_____

_____

_____

_____

_____

_____

_____

_____

_____

INTEGRITY

– does integrity play a role in your daily life?

_____

_____

_____

_____

_____

_____

_____

_____

_____

_____

WHERE DO YOU GO WHEN YOU JUST NEED TO GET AWAY?

_____

_____

_____

_____

_____

_____

_____

_____

_____

_____

_____

_____

_____

_____

_____

_____

_____

_____

_____

Use this acrostic to consider how you could
demonstrate humility in your life.

H _____

U _____

M _____

B _____

L _____

E _____

What makes you totally unique?

_____

_____

_____

_____

_____

_____

_____

_____

_____

_____

_____

"You will know the truth, and the truth will set you free."

JOHN 8:32 ESV

_____

_____

_____

_____

_____

_____

_____

_____

_____

_____

_____

_____

> **EVER ENCOURAGING,
> OUR GOD BECKONS US:
> COME TO ME. YOU CAN MAKE IT.
> YOU'RE ALMOST THERE.**

_____

_____

_____

_____

_____

_____

_____

_____

_____

_____

What does it look like for you to honor your parents?

_____

_____

_____

_____

_____

_____

_____

_____

_____

_____

_____

What things are most concerning in this season?
Can you reflect on the bigger picture and
set your heart on future glory?

_____

_____

_____

_____

_____

_____

_____

_____

_____

_____

_____

_____

What do you think are your greatest strengths?

_____

_____

_____

_____

_____

_____

_____

_____

_____

_____

_____

Hope starts with the promises of God.

Whether you work outside the home or at home, there have to be some things you love about your current job. Name five.

1. _____

2. _____

3. _____

4. _____

5. _____

The most powerful force in the universe is also
the most gentle. How can you grasp hold of
God's powerful love today?

_____

_____

_____

_____

_____

_____

_____

_____

_____

_____

_____

WHAT DOES GRACE LOOK LIKE TO YOU?

_____

_____

_____

_____

_____

_____

_____

_____

_____

_____

_____

BELIEVE
– what do you truly believe?

_____

_____

_____

_____

_____

_____

_____

_____

_____

Truthful words will stand the test of time,
but one day every lie will be seen for what it is.

PROVERBS 12:19 TPT

_____

_____

_____

_____

_____

_____

_____

_____

_____

_____

_____

When do you feel most aware
of God's presence?

_____

_____

_____

_____

_____

_____

_____

_____

_____

_____

On a scale of 1 to 10, how relaxed do you feel today?

1 2 3 4 5 6 7 8 9 10

_____

_____

_____

_____

_____

_____

_____

_____

_____

_____

_____

Do you feel like you are owed a platform?
How can you choose love over your opinions today?

_____

_____

_____

_____

_____

_____

_____

_____

_____

_____

_____

What are your priorities in life right now?

_____

_____

_____

_____

_____

_____

_____

_____

_____

_____

_____

> TIME GIVES US BETTER PERSPECTIVE ON THE TRUE DEFINITION OF BEAUTY. SPENDING TIME WITH THOSE WE LOVE AFFORDS US A GLIMPSE INTO THE DEPTH OF BEAUTY THAT LIES WITHIN.

_____

_____

_____

_____

_____

_____

_____

_____

_____

_____

We are vessels without lids, made to overflow so God's joy can be seen by everyone. Do you need to be filled up today? What's the best way for that to happen?

_____

_____

_____

_____

_____

_____

_____

_____

_____

_____

_____

_____

How can you build your spiritual house
on a solid foundation?

_____

_____

_____

_____

_____

_____

_____

_____

_____

_____

_____

_____

Give thanks in all circumstances; for this is
the will of God in Christ Jesus for you.

1 THESSALONIANS 5:18 ESV

_____

_____

_____

_____

_____

_____

_____

_____

_____

_____

It has been said that home is where your heart is. What are five things you love about your home—wherever that is to you right now.

1. _____

2. _____

3. _____

4. _____

5. _____

TODAY IS
A NEW DAY,
FULL OF
PROMISE
AND LIFE.

WHAT HAVE YOU WORKED
REALLY HARD TO BE?

_____

_____

_____

_____

_____

_____

_____

_____

_____

_____

IF WE CAN LEARN TO FULLY TRUST GOD, HE WILL CALM
OUR FEARS AND STILL OUR QUICKENED HEARTS.

_____

_____

_____

_____

_____

_____

_____

_____

_____

_____

_____

How do you want to be remembered?

_____

_____

_____

_____

_____

_____

_____

_____

_____

_____

_____

GRACE

– how can you demonstrate grace today?

_____

_____

_____

_____

_____

_____

_____

_____

_____

_____

What are you putting your time, energy, and talents into?
Are they being used for God's glory?

_____

_____

_____

_____

_____

_____

_____

_____

_____

_____

_____

What does a typical day look like for you?

_____

_____

_____

_____

_____

_____

_____

_____

_____

_____

_____

We know that in all things God works for the good of those who love him, who have been called according to his purpose.

ROMANS 8:28 NIV

_____

_____

_____

_____

_____

_____

_____

_____

_____

_____

_____

> "WHEN YOU SPEND TIME WITH GOD, THERE IS NO NEED TO HIDE. YOU CAN BE EXACTLY WHO YOU ARE. YOU CAN SAY EVERYTHING YOU WANT TO SAY. THERE IS FREEDOM IN HIS PRESENCE."

_____

_____

_____

_____

_____

_____

_____

_____

_____

WHAT IS SOMETHING NEW YOU HAVE LEARNED FROM GOD'S WORD RECENTLY?

_____

_____

_____

_____

_____

_____

_____

_____

_____

_____

_____

_____

On a scale of 1 to 10, how special do you feel today?

1 2 3 4 5 6 7 8 9 10

_____

_____

_____

_____

_____

_____

_____

_____

_____

_____

Do you ever laugh so hard your cheeks hurt?
What are five things that make you
laugh like that?

1.
_____

2.
_____

3.
_____

4.
_____

5.
_____

What recent experience has made you feel deeply loved?

_____

_____

_____

_____

_____

_____

_____

_____

_____

_____

When was the last time someone went out of their way to
be nice to you? How did it make you feel?

_____

_____

_____

_____

_____

_____

_____

_____

_____

_____

_____

HOW COULD YOU BETTER
MANAGE YOUR TIME?

_____

_____

_____

_____

_____

_____

_____

_____

_____

_____

_____

_____

GOD LOVES YOU WITH A

FIERCELY PROTECTIVE,

ETERNALLY FAITHFUL,

INESCAPABLE LOVE.

If anyone longs to be wise, ask God for wisdom and he will give it!

JAMES 1:5 TPT

_____

_____

_____

_____

_____

_____

_____

_____

_____

_____

_____

_____

Use this acrostic to consider how you could gain wisdom and understanding.

S
_____

M
_____

A
_____

R
_____

T
_____

CONFIDENCE

– where does your confidence lie today?

_____

_____

_____

_____

_____

_____

_____

_____

_____

_____

What is the most amazing thing you have experienced lately?

_____

_____

_____

_____

_____

_____

_____

_____

_____

_____

_____

Write down three mistakes you've made and then list
what those mistakes have taught you.

MISTAKE

1. _____

_____

_____

2. _____

_____

_____

3. _____

_____

_____

LESSON

1. _____

_____

_____

2. _____

_____

_____

3. _____

_____

_____

> **TRAIN YOUR HEART TO RUN FIRST TO GOD WITH YOUR PAIN, JOY, FRUSTRATION, AND EXCITEMENT. HIS FRIENDSHIP WILL NEVER LET YOU DOWN!**

_____

_____

_____

_____

_____

_____

_____

_____

_____

_____

DO YOU FEEL THE NEED TO ALWAYS BE PREPARED? WHY OR WHY NOT?

_____

_____

_____

_____

_____

_____

_____

_____

_____

_____

_____

If you had all the courage in the world,
what are five things you would do?

1. _____

2. _____

3. _____

4. _____

5. _____

What is stopping you from sharing God's good news with others? How can you take down that barrier?

_____

_____

_____

_____

_____

_____

_____

_____

_____

_____

_____

Write about something that changed your life significantly.

_____

_____

_____

_____

_____

_____

_____

_____

_____

_____

_____

Let's not get tired of doing what is good. At just the right time we will reap a harvest of blessing if we don't give up.

GALATIANS 6:9 NLT

_____

_____

_____

_____

_____

_____

_____

_____

_____

_____

_____

On a scale of 1 to 10, how inspired do you feel today?

WHAT FASCINATES YOU ABOUT GOD'S CREATION?

_____

_____

_____

_____

_____

_____

_____

_____

_____

_____

_____

Waiting is not easy, but it's often worth it.
What has been worth the wait for you?

_____

_____

_____

_____

_____

_____

_____

_____

_____

_____

God is
faithful
to the
deepest
needs
of your
heart.

What story in the Bible captures your attention? Why?

_____

_____

_____

_____

_____

_____

_____

_____

_____

_____

_____

_____

_____

> **YOUR PATH HAS BEEN CHOSEN AND YOUR FEET HAVE BEEN SET UPON IT. TRULY, IT IS A PATH OF LOVE AND FAITHFULNESS.**

_____

_____

_____

_____

_____

_____

_____

_____

_____

HOPE

– what are you hoping for today?

_____

_____

_____

_____

_____

_____

_____

_____

_____

What would you love to do with your life?

_____

_____

_____

_____

_____

_____

_____

_____

_____

_____

_____

Who do you typically feel compassion toward?
Can you extend compassion today?

_____

_____

_____

_____

_____

_____

_____

_____

_____

_____

_____

_____

Time is often our greatest inhibitor. If
time were unlimited, what would you do?

_____

_____

_____

_____

_____

_____

_____

_____

_____

_____

_____

HOW DO YOU BELIEVE GOD SEES YOU?

_____

_____

_____

_____

_____

_____

_____

_____

_____

_____

_____

God revives, rebuilds, recovers, and renews. He takes what was, strips it away, and creates something completely new. How do you feel like a new person?

_____

_____

_____

_____

_____

_____

_____

_____

_____

_____

_____

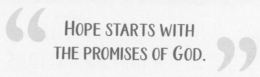

HOPE STARTS WITH THE PROMISES OF GOD.

_____

_____

_____

_____

_____

_____

_____

_____

_____

_____

_____

WHAT IS ONE OF THE BIGGEST TRANSFORMATIONS YOU HAVE BEEN THROUGH?

_____

_____

_____

_____

_____

_____

_____

_____

_____

_____

Those who hope in the LORD will renew their strength.
They will soar on wings like eagles; they will run and not grow weary,
they will walk and not be faint.

ISAIAH 40:31 NIV

_____

_____

_____

_____

_____

_____

_____

_____

_____

_____

_____

_____

When you recognize that you belong to God,
trusting him with everything becomes your new normal.
Where is God leading you today?

_____

_____

_____

_____

_____

_____

_____

_____

_____

_____

_____

_____

Do you find it easy to trust people? Why or why not?

_____

_____

_____

_____

_____

_____

_____

_____

_____

_____

_____

_____

On a scale of 1 to 10, how encouraged do you feel today?

(1) (2) (3) (4) (5) (6) (7) (8) (9) (10)

_____

_____

_____

_____

_____

_____

_____

_____

_____

_____

_____

YOUR BEST LINE OF DEFENSE IS TO SURROUND YOURSELF WITH THE TRUTH.

What is one of the hardest things
you've ever had to do?

_____

_____

_____

_____

_____

_____

_____

_____

_____

_____

_____

WONDER

– what can you stop and be in awe of today?

_____

_____

_____

_____

_____

_____

_____

_____

_____

_____

Getting a literal breath of fresh air
is great for your health! What are five things
you love to do outside?

1. _____

2. _____

3. _____

4. _____

5. _____

Where do you feel God is leading your next step?

_____

_____

_____

_____

_____

_____

_____

_____

_____

_____

_____

> GOD DOESN'T TAKE A STAB IN THE DARK WHEN YOU ARE APPROACHING HIM, GUESSING A NAME AND HOPING HE GETS IT RIGHT. HE KNOWS EXACTLY WHO YOU ARE AND WHY YOU ARE COMING TO HIM.

_____

_____

_____

_____

_____

_____

_____

_____

_____

_____

Use this acrostic to consider how you could find courage in the face of fear.

B
_____

R
_____

A
_____

V
_____

E
_____

WHAT MOTIVATES YOU
TO LEARN MORE ABOUT GOD?

_____

_____

_____

_____

_____

_____

_____

_____

_____

_____

_____

Stand on the promise that there is nothing in your history—no past or present sin—that can separate you from God's love. Can you believe your total acceptance in God?

_____

_____

_____

_____

_____

_____

_____

_____

_____

_____

_____

If your faith remains strong, even while surrounded by life's difficulties,
you will continue to experience the untold blessings of God!

JAMES 1:12 TPT

_____

_____

_____

_____

_____

_____

_____

_____

_____

_____

_____

How do you usually face your fears?

_____

_____

_____

_____

_____

_____

_____

_____

_____

_____

_____

What situations facing you right now cause you to want to run away and hide? Can you see God's hand in those situations and trust in his perfect plan?

_____

_____

_____

_____

_____

_____

_____

_____

_____

_____

_____

JOY

– where is the depth of your joy found today?

_____

_____

_____

_____

_____

_____

_____

_____

_____

_____

When do you find it
most difficult to be patient?

_____

_____

_____

_____

_____

_____

_____

_____

_____

_____

_____

Desire without hope is empty, but together they bring joy and expectancy. What are you hoping for in this season?

_____

_____

_____

_____

_____

_____

_____

_____

_____

_____

_____

THE RICHNESS OF

God's love

IS DEEPLY

SATISFYING.

What does absolute faith
look like to you?

_____

_____

_____

_____

_____

_____

_____

_____

_____

_____

There are many magnificent wonders in nature. From butterflies to mountains, all shout of a marvelous Creator. What five things have you seen that have left you in awe of God?

1.

2.

3.

4.

5.

On a scale of 1 to 10, how passionate do you feel today?

WHAT MAKES YOU FEEL LIKE SINGING?

_____

_____

_____

_____

_____

_____

_____

_____

_____

_____

_____

> "WE DON'T LEAVE OUR JUDGMENT IN THE HANDS OF A JURY. EVEN THE MOST EXPERIENCED PROSECUTOR CAN'T MAKE A CASE AGAINST US THAT WILL LAST INTO ETERNITY. GOD KNOWS WHAT HAPPENED, AND, MORE IMPORTANTLY, HE KNOWS OUR HEARTS."

_____

_____

_____

_____

_____

_____

_____

_____

Who are you in the face of conflict?
Do you avoid apologizing in an attempt to save face?
What can you do today to humble yourself
for the sake of a restored relationship?

_____

_____

_____

_____

_____

_____

_____

_____

_____

_____

_____

When do you feel most at peace?

_____

_____

_____

_____

_____

_____

_____

_____

_____

_____

_____

Trust in the LORD with all your heart; do not depend on your own understanding. Seek his will in all you do, and he will show you which path to take.

PROVERBS 3:5-6 NLT

_____

_____

_____

_____

_____

_____

_____

_____

_____

_____

_____

BEAUTY

– how do you display beauty in your life?

_____

_____

_____

_____

_____

_____

_____

_____

_____

_____

What has surprised you most in life?

_____

_____

_____

_____

_____

_____

_____

_____

_____

_____

_____

God has created us each with a unique skill set.
How can you use your gifts to benefit the church,
the community, and the world?

_____

_____

_____

_____

_____

_____

_____

_____

_____

_____

_____

_____

Write down three lies you find yourself believing.
Then list the truth.

LIE	TRUTH
1. _____	1. _____
_____	_____
_____	_____
2. _____	2. _____
_____	_____
_____	_____
3. _____	3. _____
_____	_____
_____	_____

What does a life of unconditional love look like to you?

_____

_____

_____

_____

_____

_____

_____

_____

_____

_____

_____

What five random acts of kindness could you see yourself completing in the next few weeks?

1. _____

2. _____

3. _____

4. _____

5. _____

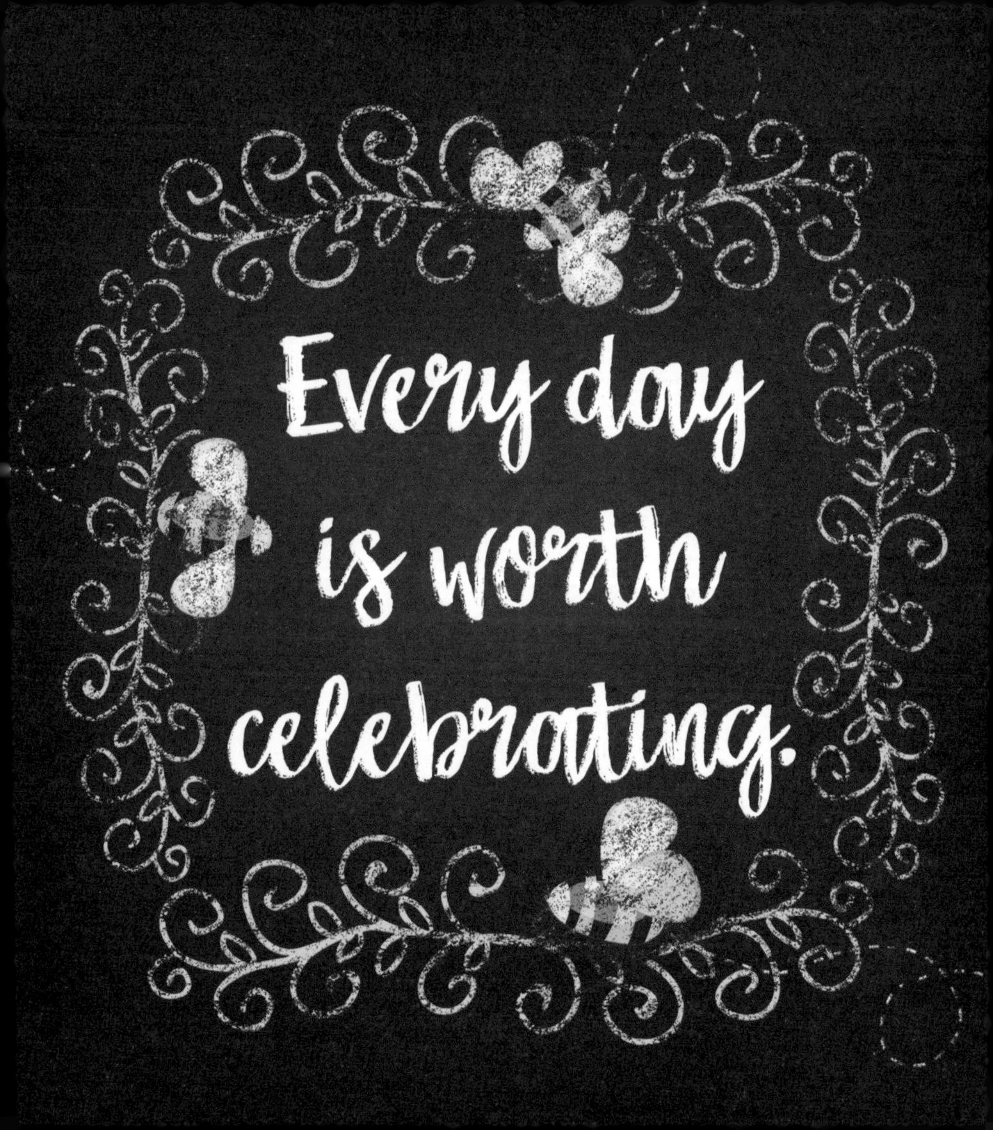
Every day
is worth
celebrating.

WHAT IS YOUR FAVORITE TIME OF THE DAY? WHY?

_____

_____

_____

_____

_____

_____

_____

_____

_____

_____

_____

Our thoughts determine our actions and our words.
What thoughts govern your mind?

_____

_____

_____

_____

_____

_____

_____

_____

_____

_____

_____

> WE LOVE TO THE DEGREE THAT WE UNDERSTAND GOD'S LOVE FOR US.

_____

_____

_____

_____

_____

_____

_____

_____

_____

_____

_____

_____

If you could ask God one question, what would it be?

_____

_____

_____

_____

_____

_____

_____

_____

_____

_____

_____

_____

On a scale of 1 to 10, how appreciated do you feel today?

(1) (2) (3) (4) (5) (6) (7) (8) (9) (10)

_____

_____

_____

_____

_____

_____

_____

_____

_____

_____

"Be strong and courageous. Do not be afraid; do not be discouraged, for the LORD your God will be with you wherever you go."

JOSHUA 1:9 NIV

_____

_____

_____

_____

_____

_____

_____

_____

_____

_____

_____

What are you thankful for today?

_____

_____

_____

_____

_____

_____

_____

_____

_____

_____

_____

STRENGTH

– what do you need strength for today?

_____

_____

_____

_____

_____

_____

_____

_____

_____

_____

What work are you waiting for God to complete in you?
How can you be patient while continuing to hope
for his promises?

_____

_____

_____

_____

_____

_____

_____

_____

_____

_____

_____

_____

Where could you use a little, or a lot,
of God's strength right now?

_____

_____

_____

_____

_____

_____

_____

_____

_____

_____

_____

Use this acrostic to consider how God gives you strength in your weakness.

S _____

T _____

R _____

O _____

N _____

G _____

Who are the top five historical figures
you admire and why?

1. _____

2. _____

3. _____

4. _____

5. _____

HOW DO YOU WANT OTHERS TO SEE GOD'S BEAUTY DISPLAYED THROUGH YOUR LIFE?

_____

_____

_____

_____

_____

_____

_____

_____

_____

_____

Turn your face to the sun. Let its warmth embrace you.
God is working in all things. In what ways do you
see him moving today?

_____

_____

_____

_____

_____

_____

_____

_____

_____

_____

_____

CHOOSE TO BE

CONTENT WITH

WHAT YOU HAVE.

Have you seen the fruit
of God's promises lately?

_____

_____

_____

_____

_____

_____

_____

_____

_____

_____

_____

What five characteristics
do you love most about God?

1. _____

2. _____

3. _____

4. _____

5. _____

You have been created to enjoy all that is exquisite, beautiful, and captivating. What can you enjoy today?

_____

_____

_____

_____

_____

_____

_____

_____

_____

_____

What word is God speaking
to you in this season?

_____

_____

_____

_____

_____

_____

_____

_____

_____

_____

_____

> *AS IF ETERNITY IN HIS KINGDOM WEREN'T ENOUGH, GOD BLESSES US EACH AND EVERY DAY, WHETHER WE ACKNOWLEDGE IT OR NOT.*

_____

_____

_____

_____

_____

_____

_____

_____

_____

_____

RELAX

– how can you take a moment to relax today?

_____

_____

_____

_____

_____

_____

_____

_____

_____

_____

How do you like to spend your weekends?

_____

_____

_____

_____

_____

_____

_____

_____

_____

_____

_____

On a scale of 1 to 10, how successful do you feel today?

① ② ③ ④ ⑤ ⑥ ⑦ ⑧ ⑨ ⑩

_____

_____

_____

_____

_____

_____

_____

_____

_____

_____

_____

What are the top five things you would
love to do on a rainy day?

1. _____

2. _____

3. _____

4. _____

5. _____

HOW IS GOD BETTER THAN ANY FRIEND YOU COULD HAVE?

_____

_____

_____

_____

_____

_____

_____

_____

_____

_____

_____

Are there people in your life that you find hard to love?
How does understanding God's love help you with this?

_____

_____

_____

_____

_____

_____

_____

_____

_____

_____

_____

There's a journey of joy in waking up every morning
knowing it's another day to breathe in the fresh air.
What moment can you find joy in today?

_____

_____

_____

_____

_____

_____

_____

_____

_____

_____

_____

In which aspect of your walk do
you feel most steady and certain?

_____

_____

_____

_____

_____

_____

_____

_____

_____

_____

_____

The season of your greatest rejoicing can be now when you consider the strength God provides.
What is worth rejoicing about today?

_____

_____

_____

_____

_____

_____

_____

_____

_____

_____

_____

Don't miss the joy of the current season by wishing it were a different one.

How can you replace frustration
with praise today?

_____

_____

_____

_____

_____

_____

_____

_____

_____

_____

_____

God delights in your voice, your laughter, and your ideas.
How do you share your life with God?

_____

_____

_____

_____

_____

_____

_____

_____

_____

_____

_____

> WHEN THE WORLD AROUND YOU SEEMS TO HAVE COLLAPSED, AND YOU FIND YOURSELF FLOUNDERING AROUND LOOKING FOR SOMETHING FIRM TO TAKE HOLD OF, GRAB GOD'S HAND. HE IS STEADY AND SURE, AND HIS LOVE IS SAFE.

ACCEPTANCE
– when do you feel most accepted?

_____

_____

_____

_____

_____

_____

_____

_____

_____

_____

What five decisions do you need to make soon?

1. _____

2. _____

3. _____

4. _____

5. _____

What are you doing right now to have the life you want?

_____

_____

_____

_____

_____

_____

_____

_____

_____

_____

_____

Establishing the right patterns begins with the renewing
of our minds. What habits are you trying to break?

_____

_____

_____

_____

_____

_____

_____

_____

_____

_____

_____

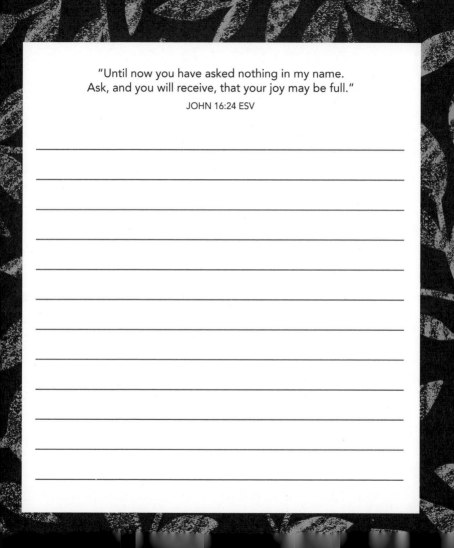

"Until now you have asked nothing in my name.
Ask, and you will receive, that your joy may be full."

JOHN 16:24 ESV

_____

_____

_____

_____

_____

_____

_____

_____

_____

_____

_____

HOW DO YOU FEEL UNDER THE LOVING GAZE OF GOD?

_____

_____

_____

_____

_____

_____

_____

_____

_____

_____

_____

_____

God created us to be relational. He knows that life is better when shared with others. How do you give yourself opportunities to be uplifted by other believers or to be an encouragement to them?

_____

_____

_____

_____

_____

_____

_____

_____

_____

_____

If we confess our sins, he is faithful and just and will
forgive us our sins and purify us from all unrighteousness.

1 JOHN 1:9 NIV

_____

_____

_____

_____

_____

_____

_____

_____

_____

_____

_____

On a scale of 1 to 10, how understood do you feel today?

(1) (2) (3) (4) (5) (6) (7) (8) (9) (10)

_____

_____

_____

_____

_____

_____

_____

_____

_____

_____

> " PRAY UNTIL THE LIFE AND POWER
> OF GOD BREAK THROUGH THE
> CLOUDS AND SHINE BRIGHTLY UPON
> YOUR FACE. HE IS ALL YOU NEED. "

_____

_____

_____

_____

_____

_____

_____

_____

_____

Use this acrostic to consider how
you could be full of life
and energy today.

L _____

I _____

F _____

E _____

True love releases past mistakes and genuinely believes for the best next time.

List five things you want to pray for regularly.

1. _____

2. _____

3. _____

4. _____

5. _____

DETERMINATION

– how determined are you today?

_____

_____

_____

_____

_____

_____

_____

_____

_____

_____

Wealth is rarely what we hope it will be; the more we have, the more we want, and the more we have to lose. Do finances consume a lot of your thoughts? Why do you think this is?

_____

_____

_____

_____

_____

_____

_____

_____

_____

_____

Write down three things you feel are impossible to accomplish. Then show how they are possible with God.

IMPOSSIBLE	POSSIBLE
1. _____ _____ _____	1. _____ _____ _____
2. _____ _____ _____	2. _____ _____ _____
3. _____ _____ _____	3. _____ _____ _____

Let the sunrise of your love end our dark night.
Break through our clouded dawn again! Only you can satisfy our
hearts, filling us with songs of joy to the end of our days.

PSALM 90:14 TPT

_____

_____

_____

_____

_____

_____

_____

_____

_____

_____

_____

How can you choose to pursue peace
in a relationship instead of being
caught up in emotions?

_____

_____

_____

_____

_____

_____

_____

_____

_____

_____

What are five things you highly value?

1. _____

2. _____

3. _____

4. _____

5. _____

When you dive into your unique life, you are saying yes to contentment and joy and moving forward into greater fulfillment and happiness. What does your unique life look like?

_____

_____

_____

_____

_____

_____

_____

_____

_____

_____